"The discovery of the fabulously rare *Azathoth and Other Horrors* by Edward Pickman Derby is a monumental achievement. Veteran editor Leigh Blackmore has added a number of poems to the original edition of 1931. Derby's poetry as a whole shows him to be a truly haunted individual—haunted by terrors in life, literature, and the boundless cosmos. There may be some danger in reading this book: beware the blasting of your soul by Derby's array of versified venom!"
– S. T. Joshi

IFWG PUBLISHING'S CHAPBOOK SERIES OF TITLES

Black Moon: Graphic Speculative Flash Fiction, by Eugen Bacon

Tool Tales: Microfiction Inspired by Antique Tools, by Kaaron Warren (photography by Ellen Datlow)

Stark Naked (poetry collection) by Silvia Cantón Rondoni

Infectious Hope: Poems of Hope and Resilience From the Pandemic, edited by Silvia Cantón Rondoni

Morace's Story (children's novella, companion to Walking the Tree) by Kaaron Warren

Songs From a White Heart (poetry collection), by Jack Dann

Sunset Tales: Haunted Tales of Africa (short fiction), by Biola Olatunde

Azathoth and Other Horrors: The Collected Nightmare Lyrics by Edward Pickman Derby, by Leigh Blackmore

AN IFWG PUBLISHING CHAPBOOK

AZATHOTH AND OTHER HORRORS

THE COLLECTED NIGHTMARE LYRICS BY EDWARD PICKMAN DERBY

EDITED BY LEIGH BLACKMORE

(A POETRY COLLECTION BY LEIGH BLACKMORE)

Internal art: copyright © Gavin L. O'Keefe
Cover art and design: Luke Spooner

IFWG Publishing International
Gold Coast
www.ifwgpublishing.com

DEDICATION

This volume is dedicated to Derrick Hussey for his ongoing support of the genre of weird poetry via the bi-annual journal *Spectral Realms*, published by Hippocampus Press and to S.T. Joshi for his perspicacious editing in the field.

Also to my fellow Australian weird poets—Charles Danny Lovecraft, Kyla Lee Ward, and David Schembri.

ACKNOWLEDGEMENTS

To R. Alain Everts, for publishing my earliest weird verse.

I would also like to acknowledge the following for their assistance with various aspects of this publication: Gerry Huntman, Fred Phillips, Luke Spooner, Richard L. Tierney (R.I.P.).

TABLE OF CONTENTS

FOREWORD

SHADOWS AND MARVELS: THE WEIRD VERSE OF EDWARD PICKMAN DERBY

The recent rediscovery of a copy of the rare volume of poetry, *Azathoth And Other Horrors* by Edward Pickman Derby (1890-1933), long thought lost, is exceptionally exciting. Derby's collection of weird verse provides frissons of the supernatural and the cosmic which will delight the souls of all devotees of the unusual and all cognoscenti of the macabre. Written in a time before Jack Kerouac observed the red stars of Azathoth, Derby's poetry is both redolent of bohemia and brimful of primal chaos.

Derby's legendary volume ranks in scarcity with such volumes of decadently macabre verse as Count Stenbock's *Love, Sleep and Dreams: A Volume Of Verse* (Oxford: A. Thomas Shrimpton & Son; Simpkin Marshall and Co, 1881); *Myrtle, Rue And Cypress: A Book Of Poems, Songs And Sonnets* (London: Hatchards, 1883); and *The Shadow Of Death: Poems, Songs, And Sonnets* (London: The Leadenhall Press, 1893); David Park Barnitz's *The Book of Jade* (1901; reprinted in 2010—NY: Hippocampus Press); and Justin Geoffrey's *The People of the Monolith* (c. 1918).

A cohort of modern scholars remain convinced that Edward Pickman Derby never actually existed in reality. The current text powerfully refutes their position. Derby posed as a decadent, trying to be as much of a Rimbaud, Baudelaire, Dowson or Lautreamont as he could, in a time of the Flapper and the Charleston.

Eighteen is a young age at which to be capable of producing verses of the quality found herein. But Derby, both a precocious child and an autodidact, was an immense intellect.

Because it was published when Derby was but eighteen, *Azathoth and Other Horrors* reminds us irresistibly of the volume *The Star-Treader and Other Poems* (1912), by Clark Ashton Smith. The young Smith was the protégé of George Sterling. The older poet assisted Smith, at the tender age of nineteen, to publish his first volume of verse. The result was international acclaim and highly favourable reviews from American critics, even leading to Smith being dubbed "the Keats of the Pacific" by one prominent reviewer. Derby's volume had a more chequered reception. On publication, it caused quite the stir, being received with considerable dismay amongst Derby's immediate circle at Miskatonic University. In the wider literary community, however, it was scarcely reviewed.

Derby issued his book in an edition of only 100 numbered copies. He presented No 2 to his friend Daniel Upton, keeping the copy numbered '1' for himself. No copies are known to exist other than No 2, which has now come to light. Indeed, not a single copy is listed on Worldcat, the online catalog of books in libraries worldwide. Perhaps a few lie mouldering in dusty attics in Arkham, or still reside in private hands elsewhere.

Rescued from Oblivion: The Discovery of the Text

It appears that Derby's friend Daniel Upton, who possessed a copy of the book presented to him (inscribed) by Derby, passed it on, in turn, to his own son, Edward Derby Upton. The copy from which the text herein has been prepared came to light a few years ago, in an internet auction of the effects of the late Edward D. Upton. The inscription on its title page reads: "For my friend Daniel Upton, in fond memory of those many conversations we have shared regarding the Dark—with all kind wishes, Edward Derby." The inscription is in dark blue ink, most likely from a fountain pen, in flowing yet erratic script, and is undated. Along with the first edition of the volume came a sheaf of manuscript papers. These proved to be originals of the later poems by Derby which are printed here.

Little enough is known of the real Edward Pickman Derby save the scant facts recorded in Lovecraft's famed ficto-critical account "The Thing on the Doorstep" 1933 (TD) where Lovecraft used considerable artistic license in his portrayal of the real-life Derby. The poet's friend, Daniel Upton, was about 28 years old during the events as related in that account. Upton was six years senior to Edward Pickman Derby, thus Derby must have been aged around 22 at that time. And thus the events of that tale take place primarily in 1935—four years after the 1931 publication of *Azathoth and Other Horrors*.

Azathoth and Other Horrors was issued by Miskatonic University Press, Arkham, in 1931. The book was one of those slim, gilt volumes liable to be issued by young poets, especially those of the fin-de-siecle and Symbolist period by which Edward Pickman Derby was heavily influenced. Since we know from Lovecraft's account that the poet was in his eighteenth year when his book was issued, it follows that Derby must have been born in 1912 (i.e. just prior to World War I). We have reason to believe he had begun to compose verse at age seven—that is by around 1919. Lovecraft wrote of Derby, through the character of his friend Upton: "He was the most phenomenal child scholar I have ever known, and at seven was writing verse of a sombre, fantastic, almost morbid cast which astonished the tutors." (TD).

Lovecraft's characterization of Edward Derby is a complex amalgam. Space here precludes detailing it extensively, but the depiction of Derby as a secluded, coddled child prodigy in "The Thing on the Doorstep" owes much to Lovecraft's own autobiography. Too, Lovecraft appears to have modelled his version of Derby upon Clark Ashton Smith, for his exotic and similarly-titled poetry; and Frank Belknap Long, for his inability to grow a beard. Another possible model is Alfred Galpin, a friend of Lovecraft's who was eleven years his junior, whom Lovecraft described in letters as being "immensely my superior" in intellect.

Independent sources verify that the real Edward Pickman Derby's parents had always doted on him. He had a particular reliance on them and, similarly to Lovecraft, especially on his mother. Her death sent Derby into a depression from which it took him a long time to recover. That he subsequently moved into the old Crowninshield House with his wife, Innsmouth-born Asenath Waite, and three servants whose names are unknown to us, is easily verified from local historical records in Arkham. For certain of the wilder events involving Asenath and her father, the old wizard Ephraim Waite, we only have Lovecraft's word, and separating fact from fiction in "The Thing on the Doorstep" becomes an exercise fraught with difficulty.

In Lovecraft's account, Daniel Upton's relationship with his friend Edward Derby changed abruptly after Derby became romantically involved with Asenath Waite. Apparently this was largely due to Asenath's odd reputation, her hypnotic powers and nefarious designs, and the suggestion that her father still bore some strange control over her.

Derby's weak personality is depicted as leading his behaviour to become more erratic and as Upton investigates, events spiral out of control. (Again, see TD). Later, Daniel Upton set up his own architecture practice in Arkham, designing Miskatonic University's new Administration Building and the Pickman Nuclear Lab (so Fritz Leiber's "To Arkham and the Stars" assures us). Upton's son Edward Derby Upton was born when Daniel Upton was about 28.

But we are here not primarily concerned with the biographical facts of Edward Derby and Daniel Upton's lives, but with the legacy of Derby's weird verse.

Bubbling and Blaspheming: The Current Text

It is, undeniably, thrilling enough that we are able to present here the entire text of *Azathoth & Other Horrors* as originally published. It is with considerable additional excitement that we are able to present this *expanded* edition, which adds several poems penned later in Derby's life. Regarding these latter, an intriguing possibility presents itself. Could some of these later poems (such as "A Dream of Kamog," and "Souls of Samhain") have been actually written by Asenath Waite, Derby's wife, while she was in possession of his body and mind? Or even by old Ephraim Waite, her wizard father? ("Kamog" is either Ephraim Waite's secret name in his Chesuncook coven or is possibly the name of a non-human entity that possessed him and his family).

The centrepiece of the volume is, of course, its epic title poem, "Azathoth, or: The Daemon-Sultan." One can well imagine why this poem, especially, might have caused a mild sensation amongst the small coterie of readers who had access to it on first publication, with its focus on the blind idiot god Azathoth—Lord of All Things, the amorphous blight of nethermost confusion—encircled by his flopping horde of mindless dancers, and lulled by the thin monotonous piping of a demonic flute.

The verses themselves, with their variety of form, technical precision and fluently obsessive utilisation and iteration of the themes of darkness, cosmicism, dissolution of sanity, and death, make *Azathoth & Other Horrors* a sombre gem for connoisseurs of poetic wizardry.

Some of the poems gathered here clearly derive directly from Derby's real-life experiences, early or late—see, for instance, "Arkham Sanitarium." Yet others—"Azathoth," "Shub-Niggurath," and "Shoggoths" amongst them—reflect Derby's deep reading and absorption of dark occult lore and legend.

We also see some influence from the notorious Baudelairian poet Justin Geoffrey, a close friend of Edward Pickman Derby and with whom Derby actually corresponded. Geoffrey published his *The People of the Monolith* after visiting the sinister, ill-regarded Hungarian village of Stregoicavar and died "screaming in a madhouse." He was remembered by the villagers as acting in an odd manner, with a habit of mumbling to himself. Derby chose to dedicate the poem "With Wizard Way" to Justin Geoffrey, of whom we know even less than of Derby, though Geoffrey receives mention in the Robert E. Howard tale "The Black Stone" (1931).

One hopes that the republication of the bulk of Edward Derby's verse will establish him anew as a significant figure in weird literature, despite the considerable personal costs that have been entailed to the wellbeing of your editor in compiling this disturbing material. Come with me now, as Edward Pickman Derby does his part to drag the world down a black spiral vortex to the central void where the daemon sultan Azathoth gnaws hungrily in the dark…

Footnote: Two other poems have been published under Derby's name in modern times. These are "Azathoth," in Robert M. Price's *The Azathoth Cycle: Tales of the Blind Idiot God* (Oakland, CA; Chaosium, March 1995), where it appeared 'by permission of the agent for the author's estate, Vartan Bagdasarian.' This extended piece of verse laid claim to being the very title poem of Derby's famous volume. The second piece allegedly by Derby, and published under his name, was "The Philtre," a much shorter piece which appeared in *Crypt of Cthulhu* Vol 19, No 2 (Whole Number 104) (Eastertide 2000), published by Mythos Books. It is now known that both these poems, from the same hand, are spurious, and do not derive from Derby's original publication—a fact which examination of the original 1931 text upon which the current volume is based makes clear. Evidently they were written by a talented modern pasticheur who wishes to remain unidentified. His identity is known to the current editor, but a discreet veil shall be drawn over it.

LEIGH BLACKMORE
Wollongong NSW Australia
5 October 2023

THE ADVERSE STAR

Unclouded moon lofts high above the bar
And seems to sigh and signal where you are;
It is a thing unseemly and bizarre,
The rulership of this most Adverse Star

That blinks beside the moon and casts wan light
From gulphs uncrossed, and makes your skin glow white.
The Adverse Star is glinting there this night;
I wish it were not half so deathly bright!

The fateful course that set us on our way
Has taken us from hearth and home; dismay
And lost desire; storm-wrack blots the day
In motionless embrace; all seems passé.

The cracks of time now in our voices are
As we lament the heavenly vision far
And strum our sad and lonely old guitar
Beneath the baleful light—that Adverse Star!

WHEN THE NIGHTWIND HOWLS

He dreamt of realms forsaken
Beneath swart midnight skies;
Of men by dooms o'ertaken,
And lovers' joyful cries.

He glimpsed far Nithon's flowers;
Weird blooms he sang in note
As though from distant bowers
Where nightingales give throat.

With velvet gowns and silky
That draped unearthly shapes
Of luscious maidens milky,
Reclining, eating grapes,

His visions filled his pages
With silver and with gold;
With tales of ancient ages
And heroes swift and bold;

He dreamt of worlds forgotten:
Colossal planets, vast;
And creatures ill-begotten
From aeons, ages past;

And when we hear the nightwind
A-howling in the eaves,
And when the full noon turns dusk-dimmed,
His muse will make blood freeze.

He sang far lands and starlight;
He sang weird loves obsessed;
And when we sense a far light
We think long on his quest

To bring the realms of fancy
Within each reader's grasp—
He penned dark necromancy
In lines that make us gasp.

His wizardry is ended—
His magic though, lives on.
His course, though now it's wended
Will never be quite gone.

THE SILENT SILVER SEA

The sea of silent silver lies
Where pockmarked moons ride purple skies.
Here once, my long-lost love with me
Stood, rapturous, near that silver sea.

The silent, silvern sea spreads calm.
I walk its shore 'neath fronded palm,
Remembering my love, how we
Clasped close beside that silent sea.

The soundless, silver sea recedes
Horizonwards, as it proceeds
Upon its way; we were so free
When walking by that soundless sea.

By soundless, silvern sea we loved
And by our vows our love we proved,
So long ago. Oh, set me free!
Can she yet live near silver sea?

Near silvern, silent sea we pledged
Undying love, near seaside edged
With flotsam, jetsam; so carefree
Were we beside that silent sea.

That silent, silver, soundless sea!
I failed to know, did not foresee
Her leaving; knew not what would be
The ending of our love, and me.

No clasping close! No pledge of love!
No vows or freedom with my Dove!
Is all that now remains to me—
The silent, silver, soundless sea?

The silver sea, it seems to sigh.
Is that my love returning nigh
As waves recede and then return?
What tidal secret may I learn?

For love eternal by that sea
Was promised between her and me;
And in my dreams she lays her hands
Upon my brow on those strange sands.

A ghost or real? What can it be
That I behold near silent sea?
My soul cries out! Shall I be free?
Though it may be but fantasy,

She soon returns beside me here—
Her body pale, so close, so near
That I can sense her trembling form
Within the sea, within the storm.

That silvern sea, no sound it makes
As sanity gives way and breaks
Like waves and foam. A final plea
I make unto the silver sea!

LIKE SCARLET WINE

Ablaze with gold the fresh and virgin day
That heralds all the promise of your kiss;
Awash with amber light upon my way,
I step into a world where naught's amiss.

Like molten wax your burning heart on mine—
Like veins that run with mercury and fire—
Like arms that clasp and hold, like scarlet wine—
Like these things are the depths of our desire.

A melody upon my lips is you;
The birdsong in the trees thrills too within.
Embracing you I see the world anew—
In loving you I know that I can win.

LAMIA

The lapidary lamia's lifetime .
Is spent a-crouch in lair of wet, black caves.
She curls her tail about her in the slime—
Seductress, harlot—her rough skin she laves.

Hetaira of the sovereign night, she waits
With horrent hairs upon her serpent tail—
A filthy glutton, made so by the Fates—
Enchantress, witch, Zeus-cursed one—white and pale,

Wide eyes unclosing, face twisted awry.
This odalisque of horror lures a child
Within her reach. Its piteous dying cry
Rings out, its life by succubus defiled.

This vampire daemon, almondine of eye,
Malevolent dark haunter of the night,
Bides awful time. Libyan Queen descry—
All humans perish here beneath her sight.

SHOGGOTHS

Whence dreaded Ubbo-Sathla came, they come
These protoplasmic beings of vast size;
The depths of earth's dim caverns they will plumb;
They probe the dark with glistening great eyes

That form and re-form, myriads on their skins.
Self-luminous and shapeless, black as slime,
Their iridescent, evil, alien grins
Grow shapeless as they slither out of time.
These mutant congeries—like Elder Things—
Pustules in motion, trailing foetid strings!

SHADOWLANDS

My head is filled with skeleton trees;
My thoughts are full of skeleton keys;
Trees nod their skulls like skeleton men;
The road is rough and stardark again.

Lovesick, I see you stand still and fair,
Mired deep in mud. With black branches bare,
Tall trees glow bright and unearthly-hued;
Dim peaks rise far, with shadows imbued.

Your hair is twined with skeleton bones;
You dream of kings on skeleton thrones;
Your dress of shadows conceals your form;
Your face, anguish-lit, is split by storm.

I feel the beat of skeleton heart;
I drag my feet. There is some black art
At work; I feel its skeleton bane
Pour forth to waste my pitiful brain.

My ears are filled with skeleton cries;
Your lips, they part; 'neath menacing skies
I see my fate; you raise your clawed hands—
"Beware, beware, the dread Shadowlands!"

WITH WIZARD WAY

(FOR JUSTIN GEOFFREY)

With wizard way did ancient Mage
Enact strange spells of fire and air;
He wrote with blood on vellum page
Dark runes from out an Elder Age,
And banished spirits from their lair
Within his temple censed with sage;

For conjuration on the chalk-drawn ground
Weird, eldritch, arcane symbols circled round.
And here were consecrated weapons true—
The Wand, the Vessel, Pentacle and Sword.
The Mage knew all their functions; as he grew
In stature for the rite, he now was Lord

Of consecrated space. In light aslant,
A roaring evocation ancient—
His words of power rang forth like plainchant
To summon up the daemon—to implant
His Will upon the creature and enchant
It here and now to do his lawful bidding!
As if the fires of Hell were loathe, forbidding,
The daemon did not come at once, but tarried.
And so the Mage spoke louder as he harried
That denizen of Hell in voice like thunder:
"Appear before me, here and now, O fiend!"
In flames the daemon came and as it keened
Its cry, it sank before him; kneeled there under
His magisterial sway. "I now command

That thou shalt be full subject unto me!
That whether on the Earth or on dry Land
Upon the Earth or flailing in the Sea,
In whirling Air or rushing Fire thou trod,
That thou obey each Spell and Scourge of God!"

Ensorcellment profound! That evocation
That gripped the daemon dread in searing blast!
Enshackled now with potent imprecation—
It served the Mage; would ever be steadfast!

AZATHOTH,
OR: THE DAEMON-SULTAN

"It is a tale told by an idiot, full of sound and fury, signifying
nothing"– Shakespeare, *Macbeth*

A whining wind drives wraiths of cloud about,
Arousing terror in my nervous soul.
I cannot sleep; the moon is choked; I shout
In darkness direful, black as any coal.

Metallic ghosts are spread upon the lake,
Dim mists that hover, white, opaque and still;
And in my room the air is clogged; I quake,
All veiled and steeped in dark; my flesh is chill.

A candle guttering in darkness here
Seems like my life, so pitiful and small;
Though I am now once more in Earthly sphere,
I fear the things that swarm and squirm and crawl.

Abysmal voids have opened to my feet;
Atrocious gulfs have swallowed all my sense;
And though for now returned to my own street
I fear those shifting spaces so immense.

Harsh age had fallen on the ugly world;
Wonder had gone from out the human heart;
Grey cities reared and smoky skies unfurled
Tall towers grim, from beauty set apart.

The shadow of those towers starved our dreams
Of sun and moon and fanciful witch-elms,

The flowering meads of Spring and sunlight beams
And visions vast of wondrous cosmic realms.

Rote knowledge stripped the Earth of comely wealth
And poets sang no more of golden corn.
They sang of twisted phantoms, of ill-health,
With inward vision bleared and voices worn.

When childish hopes had flown away for good
And all these ills had fallen on the Earth
I travelled out of life—I knew I could—
Upon a quest for charms that were in dearth.

It was a quest into the spaces far
Whither the world's bright dreams had flowed and fled.
By day I dwelt and toiled beneath the scar
Of that drear city where I made my bed.

I toiled in shadow; turmoil was my lot
Until the sterile, twilight evening fell.
I knew no groves nor fields in that grey spot—
But just a court wherein the light did well

To penetrate, and windows blind despaired.
From my one casement, nothing but the wall
And shutters could be seen; a lone star glared
When I leaned out, peered far aloft. In thrall

That sole star held me every dreadful night
As I delved deep, absorbed obscure lore
And dreamed much that was bound to fast ignite
The madness in my soul; I did implore

The chaos in my mirror to come forth.
It was the glass of Erich Zann, now mine;
From Rue d'Auseil it came. Both South and North
Had once paid homage to its grim design

And awesome power. Beyond dimensioned space
It offered glimpses strange—black voids alive
With motion and with music—things no face
Beheld without loss of the will to thrive.

Illimitable space! No semblance there
Of anything on earth that lives or breathes!
And lost in endless dream I made my prayer
Into the glass, unto the Thing that seethes!

Slow-sailing stars, I knew them all by name
And followed them in fancy when they hid,
Until—at length—my inner eye became
Accustomed to their secrets; and they bid

Me do dark deeds and formless acts of chance.
Dream-haunted skies swelled down and slowly merged
Within my room's close airs. A dark romance
Of cosmic wonder had me deep submerged—

And then flowed forth the violet midnight streams—
Wild midnight glittering all with dust of gold—
Strange vortices of dusk and fire and dreams
From spaces perfumed…over me they rolled!

Now opiate oceans poured into my room—
Sun-litten by weird suns without a name
That lit the space and drove away the gloom
And having in their whirlpools dolphins tame

And sea-nymphs, unrememberably deep.
My body from the window stiffly leaned
As noiseless eddies, space-flown, made me sleep
And whirled and wafted me; it was some fiend

Which had me in its grip and bore me out
For countless days unto the farthest spheres.
I sought the visions men have dreamed about;
Instead, the fiend would show me only fears.

I longed on sunrise shores so green to sleep,
On shores with fragrant lotos-blossoms strewn,
But mindless rhythms drew me to the deep
Of aimless angled space, where to the tune

Of muffled flutes' accursed alien whine
There lives a Thing—a blind idiot God
Created by the cosmos, Byzantine,

As joke or jest; and only few have trod

The ways toward this Lord of Mindless Void.
This Chaos Ultimate that gives the lie
To humankind's illusion, now destroyed
Of self-importance. Now, to horrify,

Great Azathoth, a monstrous nuclear force—
Malign, age-old, destructive—holds His sway
Amidst the drums that pulse with rhythm coarse
Played monstrously by paws of grim decay.

I see Him now, as I am whirled apace
Through blackest night; the brilliant stars shine down.
Colossally the foul, aged Chaos Face
Looms large upon my sight; I fear the frown

Of festering dim horrors as they float
About the central void; my soul is chilled
The idiot vortices grow fat and bloat
As yet I tumble; will my life be stilled?

Abomination this! Great Outer Gods!
This Daemon-Sultan on His horrid throne
Gnaws hungry—*live*, despite all mortal odds!
Thin high cracked flutes that make my hearing stone!

Ill-favoured beasts disport around the Thing—
Strange, shapeless, bat-winged, ghastly to behold!
I fall and tumble further as I cling
To sanity's last shreds. Infernal cold!

The sable void and Daemon Azathoth
Fill all my vision as I spin and turn.
Unspeakably abnormal—His dark wrath
Is blasting me; my flesh begins to burn!

Flatigious God, of utter alien source!
No pity there, implacable His reign!
Dark Azathoth, inexorable force!
Can I escape, or shall I go insane?

I whirl anew in this black cosmic heart
That *Necronomicon* once lightly cloaked

With 'Azathoth' as name... At last my heart
Beats slow and true; I rue that I evoked

This desperate gambit—ghastly universe!
Damned mayhap though I be, I have escaped
The coruscating *horror* of the curse
Although my sanity is close to raped.

Through space my shattered body does return
To that small room beside the dim white lake.
Unspeakably, the life within does burn
But Azathoth my soul has failed to take.

And now, exhausted, fevered, here I lie...
To feed the body, just a little broth;
In deep relief, I utter a small cry
Of grief—at having met dread Azathoth!

ALCHEMY OF OBLIVION

(FOR CHARLES BAUDELAIRE)

With jaundiced eye you regard
The gloomy confines of this room.
The cobblestones of the court
Resound with the misery and scandal
That plague our neighbours
And indeed ourselves.

Mysterious and doomed,
This alchemy of oblivion
That hovers over us,
Perfervid and insidious,
Spurs us on to bleaker woes.

Here, in our delirious desolation
We drink in a trance of broken days,
Of bleakly tarnished hours,
Filled with wine and insolent song—
What rapture our drugs and poisons bring!
What beauty is provided
By our delicious languor
As we slowly waste away.

The mournful cries outside
Are nothing compared to the insolent sarcasm
We inflict on each other
In our shame…
We slake our thirsts with mournful forbidden musics.

The void beckons,
Yet we disdain suicide;
It would be a disgrace.
And so we spend our automatic days,
Our suffering nights,
In a profusion of hideous ecstasies,
Of alchemies of oblivion.

THE WITCHES' BOWER

From Winter's black season beneath the red moon
When tempests blow hard 'neath pale fretwork of stars,
When surly gods seem to be crying a croon
Like frogs croaking loudly and lonely nightjars,

The season is changing to bountiful Spring.
The hearts of the witches are filled with delight
As all dance in joy in their small faery ring,
And luminous boles glow in silent sunlight.

The softness and sweetness of fruit on the bough,
Made piquant with roses that bring the lovethirst,
Combine to make witches wear garlands at brow
And honour the Maid Mother Winter has nursed.

Now here in the bower, their veins beat with song
As athames, censers and candles adorn
The high sacred altar, the Spring to prolong
With chalices, ruby wine, wands and oaths sworn.

These nymphs and these satyrs who love the old Craft
And languidly cling in the bower's embrace
Chant Charge of the Goddess aloud; their witchcraft
Is truly the craft of the Wise, and of grace.
Aa petals drop quiet to make a soft bed,
The witches entwine in their love-rite so fair.
The altar with pentacle, wand and cornbread
Bears witness so silent to each witch's prayer.

And as golden evening descends on the flower
Of youthful and Crone-like together this night,
The witches raise energy, send Cones of Power
To alter the world from its wrongness to right.

IN SPLENDOUR ALL ARRAYED

Through endless starry ages have I been
As one who standing naked, unafraid,
With palms outstretched, in splendour all arrayed
Beseeches all to see what he has seen.

On alien worlds and serried dying suns
I stride as one who claims his rightful place,
Deep breathing of fresh air, with rapturous face,
Partaking of all things that have been done.

On Earth I lived, in time antique and rare,
And died, and lived again beneath grey skies,
And witnessed many things with aged eyes
That made me will, and know, and then to dare.

And in far realms unearthly have I trod,
As though with psalms, petitions and with prayer
Some strange and unknown being placed me there
And prayed to *me*, as like unto a god.

Ethereal and celestial visions throng
My fevered brain, the deathless ages pass.
I see so clearly through the sages' glass
These cosmic realms, it seems, where I belong.

THE GOBLIN GOBLET

How strangely unfamiliar is your face!
I thought I knew it once an age ago
When forms diverse trod stars above this place
Like vast and vital fire-sparks all aglow.

So pallid, ah how pallid is your face!
I know I kissed those chilly lips of yore
When magic music coursed through outer space
And made my soul your own soul to adore.

Madness and magic mingle in your face!
I swear I held it close and felt its tears
When orbs translunary saw our embrace
And poured their fire-opal on our years.

Your face is all elusive like your smile!
I wish I could remember when we loved;
E'en so I think I'll tarry here a while
With you, my strange indefinite beloved.

How gem-like is your face, that pallid face!
I think that jade and jasper once were ours
But of our pearls and rubies now no trace—
Our spirits have surrendered to grim powers.

The goblin goblet of your poisoned face
Is poised above my own, a swollen moon
Prodigious, evil, lacking in all grace,
'Twas pallid, now 'tis dusky deep maroon.

I sink beneath the presence of your face
As one bewitched, unable to transcend
Your loathsome power. And now you will erase
My being as my memory. You descend!

SHUB-NIGGURATH

What incantation vile, repugnant, foul
Has brought Her forth from hellish, darksome Wood
Wherein she reigns? All-Mother! What low growl
Of odious beast, that long and lone has stood

Awaiting Her, shall greedy greet her now?
A Thousand Young she fiercely does command!
The great Black Goat—upon her lowering brow
Nug's ghastly sigil, Yeb's bright-burning brand
Of evil fire; wordless speech it hath!
Bow down and worship! *Ia! Shub-Niggurath!*

TIME'S VULTURE

Unvanquishable Time doth swoop and sweep
To bring its presence, cause a growing gloom.
From birth to death we can but lie so deep
Within its grip of creeping, clutching doom.

Time's Vulture is a deadly bird that roams
Upon the Earth where empires fall and rise
And on the sea where emerald ocean foams
And in the sullen cloud-towers of the skies.

Nocturnal moths lie sleeping in the rust.
The Vulture's fatal, rending, red-mouthed kiss,
Makes amethystine diamonds rot to dust
And planets cease to roll in the abyss.

The full moon wanes, effaced by cruel claws
And suns of ages golden fade away;
The Vulture sinks its talons, snaps its jaws
Upon the worlds where sorrow now holds sway.

Time's Vulture hangs aloft o'er all our lives—
Its carrion wings cast shadows on the sands.
Mortality, despotic, sink its knives
Into our hearts with ultimate demands.

The hovering oblivion blights our nights
When dark thoughts prey inside our dreaming heads.
And skulls of kings bear witness to last rites
That haunted them when *they* lay in their beds.

FROZEN VOICES

The frozen voices sing a song of cold;
Deep lucent shadows steep the hillside bare—
Grim traceries upon the ancient mould
Where once there lay a palest gleam of gold.

Through soulless dusk, the freshets run so slow
'Neath crumbling bridges built in elder times.
The frozen voices rise, sing out their woe;
Insistent, clappered bells ring out their rhymes.

With hollow cheeks and eyes like dim, dark pools,
The deathless singers weary of their task.
Their litany proceeds; now these grim ghouls
Their frigid song continue like a masque,

With scanty hair and spindly limbs of ice.
The frozen singers' voices flare and fade.
In muted tones they tell the fatal price
They paid—their former lives they have betrayed.

LINES ON A DRAWING BY HANNES BOK

The waves wash out to sea with hiss and roar
Receding to horizon from the shore
Whereon the hunting figure, muscled hard,
Is striding proud, a seaweed-covered bard.

The barefoot maid he faces on the sand
Covers her breast and points her lightsome hand;
Her hair, aflame with moonlight, kissed with love,
Streams out, as does the light from stars above.

Does his grim visage portend some dark trial
Which he shall visit on her in a while?
Or is he in her thrall, her misty power
Dictating his dim fate in this late hour?

THE LOATHLY GOD

I trod the path no-one had trod
That led me deep into the wood
To find the loathly unknown god
Where crumbling moss-grown temples stood.

My fevered brain had led me here,
Far from the haunts of city folk
Where I had dwelled for many a year,
Exhaustless in my quest baroque.

It was a quest of death and night,
A search for evils yet unknown
That drove me onward, past the blight
Of normalcy; 'twas I alone

Who wished it; all my soul cried out
To know the god who secret dwelled
In that dark wood; his rites no doubt
Were recondite, though long since quelled.

With bodeful tread I moiled my way
Through strangling thickets, clutching vines—
Fared ever on, while swift the day
Sank into dusk behind the pines.

Past hippogriff and sciapod
I fought my way; I would not rest;
In sombre wonder I must plod
Undaunted—I must pass the test!

The Loathly God was known of old
To people of this hidden land;
Its face, composed of darkling mold—
So said the books that now were banned

Wherein the wizards, ages past
Had written of demonic things.
The Loathly God was nameless, past
The ken of scribes; Its folded wings

Protected gems of wondrous price—
Of ruby, jade and emeraude!
I swore to have these riches. Thrice
I swore it! Hence, now on I strode.

By furred Tsathoggua I did curse
As jungle vines encumbered me;
But with my sword I did disperse
The thickly clinging tough debris.

'gainst jaguar and wild sloth
I gamely fought, as on I fared;
And slashing through the undergrowth
At last set foot where I had dared

To travel. Here before me stood
The ghastly fane of crumbling stone
Where dwelled the God. Since my boyhood
I longed to face it all alone.

Now was my chance! I strode inside
The thing rose mighty on its plinth—
A shocking daemon! All wide-eyed,
I travelled through the labyrinth

That led from temple entrance broad
Towards the ghastly Thing that crouched—
Gems glittering at its feet—my sword
In hand as close to it I slouched.

The Loathly God reared up its form—
Great paws, great jaws, great dripping fangs…
I thrust the sword like firestorm

Into its belly; its death pangs

Were hideous to hear; it fell
Athwart the cobbles, bloody, slain;
I swept the glittering gemstones well
Into my sack like coloured rain.

The Loathly God is dead and gone—
I thank Tsathoggua every night;
And I adventure on and on…
But *why* do I still wake in fright?

THE BONELESS

Slow-crawling things move strangely through the lanes
Of twisted towns sepulchral. Scorching fires
Illume dim ashen skies. Curious strains
Of music, sung by townsfolk in weird choirs,

Rise forth to hold the rotting things at bay.
The monstrous creatures pay the songs no heed.
They slither forth, these boneless things of clay,
Like loathly worms with tongueless mouths—and feed

On humans they encounter as they roam.
Benighted blasphemies from black domains
Make leprous sojourn from their bestial home
And squirm across the vast and darkling plains!

A DREAM OF KAMOG

From legend-haunted Arkham to the woods
Of Maine, abhorrent secret lore abounds;
In wild and lonely places Things with hoods
Do execrable rites and howl strange sounds,

They bleat "Kamog! Kamog!" The altar stands
In that unholy pit in the abyss…
Five hundred wave their trembling, upraised hands
And howl atrocious things in horrid bliss!
I see the Cyclopean ruins rise—
Their complex angles sear my dreaming eyes!

SEARCHER

From regions where the mandrake grows
And, rooted up, gives vent to screams,
A searcher, from a land of snows
Comes forth, follows the frozen streams

To venture out in unknown days
Through woods entangled all with briars
And over mountains whose dark ways
Are lit by dim funereal fires.

As, driven on his tragic quest,
He gives away his gold, his jewels,
A pain burns ever in his breast;
He lives on berries and thin gruels.

He presses on towards his goal —
If he must slay the cockatrice
He does so, for he must be whole
To find his Grail, which does entice

Him ever on, midst flaring mist;
Until, exhausted, he sinks down,
Despairing that his goal is missed —
He is no hero, but a clown.

THE NIGHT IS BLACK AND WHITE

(FOR GERARD DE NERVAL)

Chimerical and strange are all my days,
Thibault my only solace, 'neath dead moons
That transit, sadly silent, as I gaze
On gods and dragons, goddesses and runes.

Long since my star has suffered an eclipse
As through the dreaming grottoes all alone
I walk brain-weary; thinking of your lips,
And your bright eyes that weep, though you are gone.

Foam-crested waves that play on trackless shores
Spray darkling droplets as my hoarse voice sighs;
Moon-maddened, I ope sombre tomb-like doors
Which clang and close behind like thund'rous skies.

Of dusk and desperation is my life—
Black sun of melancholia, heaven's void;
My splendours passed, no peace but only strife,
Impoverishment; insane, I am destroyed.

Alchemic star-blooms play around the Moon,
My footsteps fall where happiness has fled.
Descant of sorrow, sombre pagan tune
Marks out hermetic epochs in my head.

Immortal breath of life, o vault of time!
Abyss, whose depths night-dark we cannot know,
Be with me in my poor attempts at rhyme—
Through mist-wreathed groves primordial, I go.

Too much of love and frenzy have I known;
My heart beats fast as I descend to hell.
Like souls astir beneath a shell of stone,
My last lament will all my passions quell.

DOOMED CASSILDA

And hast thou seen the Yellow Sign?
The distant stars do now align
In their dimension
For Cassilda.

And strangely worn, the Pallid Mask—
What it portends she dare not ask
And madder still grows
Poor Cassilda.

Songs of Hali shall she sing
Where birds most strange do wildly wing;
Possessed and mad is
Fair Cassilda.

Yhtill and Voht, long dynasties
Carcosan and of Hyades,
Plague scattered thoughts of
Lost Cassilda.

In Demke's cloudy depths there swirls
Forgotten evil like black pearls.
Strange shadows shroud
Doomed Cassilda.

THE FANTASTIC FLAME

I dreamed I saw a flaming pillar twined
With pulsing colours, reaching to the sky—
Resplendent, awesome, glowing. In my mind
It twisted up, a million miles high.

I stood and trembled like a bird whose wings
Were fluttering in death, whose beak still gapes.
And in the flame I witnessed vanished things—
Obscure gods and unfamiliar shapes.

Beneath the steadfast stars' exotic spray
The vast, bright pillar burned with spirit rare
And forms diverse—of suns; of time; decay
Of permanence. It bore a poisoned air.

It seemed I heard mysterious music—vague,
Ethereal, indefinite and remote.
I wondered, as the forms like fiery plague
Coiled lithe within and on my psyche smote.

To tread the stars the flaming pillar tried,
Transcending all, but could not last for long;
And so its flame died down; I almost cried
As, too, died down its deadly, beauteous song.

THE TONGUELESS DEAD

(FOR THOMAS LOVELL BEDDOES)

Bleak autumn falls upon the mossy graves,
Pale flesh falls from cadavers as if flayed.
Grave-robbers there and other evil knaves
Dig up fresh corpses for the doctor's blade.

The foetid earth and roots yield to their spades.
Old, tongueless dead lie still, their skulls and bones
Abandoned by their long-gone fleshless shades.
Grave-robbers care not; now they break the stones

That bar the way and keep them from their prize—
The fat, sleek dead new-buried in their tombs.
To carry off the dead they don disguise
That hides them from the watchmen in their rooms.

Dark Death will feast, a lasting requiem
For graveyard, morgue and fatal hanging tree;
So, amply feed the appetites of them
Who would make coin from human misery.

THE GOLDEN DIADEM

(FOR ROBERT W. CHAMBERS)

I used to love to ride but then I fell;
They say I've never been the same since then.
Insane? No—prisoned in a desperate hell
In an asylum; yet I live to tell

The tale of Wilde, he of the yellow face,
Who fixed wrecked reputations on the sly.
His was a mystic, most mysterious case.
How many served him only but to die?

All waxen were his artificial ears;
He had no fingers on his crippled hand;
Yet from his lair he spread his special fears
Through city, state and all the trembling land.

My name is Hildred Castaigne and I serve
The Yellow King whose cousin close I am;
The King whose story racks on every nerve,
Whose shadow haunts sane thoughts with curse and damn

Destruction. Emperors have served the King;
Dim hints survive of what he might portend;
But my ambition high, to which I cling—
To take my rightful place, the world to mend.

The shadows gather in the fading light;
I don the white silk robe with Yellow Sign;
I well recall the awful words of fright
That echo through Carcosa's cursed line.

The diadem of diamonds and of gold
Is flashing fire—dare not tell me that
It is but bronze and paste! It is the crown
For which I suffered Wilde's demon cat!

Some say the author of the dreaded book
Had shot himself; we know that it was seized
In France by those who did not dare to look
Into its pages, lest it prove diseased.

Censured it was, denounced as devil's tool—
The King in Yellow, maddening supreme text
Of purest poison, writ to make men drool
Stupendous art—yet some would call it hexed.

The scalloped tatters of the King must hide
The fearful memory of the Pallid Mask
Whose rule is coming; while Black Stars abide
Above the lake of Hali; the dread task

Is playing out to its stupendous end.
Infection-like, the book spreads despite pleas;
Some tried to burn it. Let the whole world bend
The knee—the King and Pallid Mask appease!

King in Carcosa I shall shortly be,
And King in Hastur where Camilla screams;
O'er Demhe and Yhtill from sea to sea;
My gaoler Archer's throat slit (in my dreams).

A Dynasty Carcosan lives on yet,
I bear that truth within my blood, each vein;
And though you lock me up, please don't forget
I bite and scratch you but I'm *not insane!*

LOVE'S RUIN

Torrential rain—
    Tall trembling trees—
Storm bringing pain—
    Love's dregs and lees.

Quick lightning flash—
    A thunder crack—
Trees split and smash—
    Love comes not back.

Damp, hissing lawn—
    Cold, wind-whipped street—
And with the morn
    Love's ruin's complete.

UNDER THE TUSCAN MOON

(FOR ELIZABETH BARRETT BROWNING)

With portraits in black carven antique frames
And chambers quaint and curiously wrought
I dwell unearthly; all Pennini's games
Have failed to cheer; my sweet child's kiss is naught.

Nathaniel Hawthorne and his wife a-stroll
Have come to call; but this is not enough
Distraction for my burning, passionate soul;
The flimsy fabric of such mundane stuff

Holds not my interest; lost in idle song,
Even my husband plays as much as works.
For me, I must have fervour, blended strong,
Suffused with Spirit for my rhymes, else lurks

The threat of ennui 'neath midsummer skies,
The sinking down beneath the brooding wings
Of coming Death; this haven yet I prize
For bringing time to pen my offerings—

To summits rising on celestial planes;
To scarlet roses, as to lilies white;
To colours in the shadows. For my pains,
Hell's vespers, prayed in ink, illume the night.

As golden orb of day—irradiate
With ordinary matters—now gives way,
Life darkens into dusk. I leave my mate;
My lines live on; I live but for today.

ICE-DEMONS

Upon tall peaks caliginous and cold,
Where frost and snow perpetually lie
And gales blow hard where glaciers have rolled,
Strange shapes are glimpsed in motion up on high—

Occluded by the sheets of sleet and snow—
These dismal creatures, galling to discern.
Aphotic realms where chill winds always blow
Surround Them, as Their fierce eyes redly burn.

Abhorrent creatures formed from jagged ice—
The Wendigo, Their cousin. Mortals sleep;
Ice-demons flock, their victims to entice—
Demoniac destruction They will reap.

This night They wing, descending on the town
That spreads below, to make Their deadly raid
Against the folk who dwell there, flying down
To wreak Their icy vengeance—evil clade!

Foison enough to stab the hearts with ice
Of innocents who live their lives in peace—
Harvest of human souls to pay such price
As demons deem is owing, without cease.

Ice-demons strike! Their fiendish talons freeze
And sink into the warm flesh, heart and bone.
This sacrifice no godhead shall appease!
They fly, returning to harsh worlds of stone.

ARKHAM SANITARIUM

They cannot cage me here within this place
Of fragile walls, of people who are blind
To other worlds, to Things that have no face,
To downward-leading stairs that twist and wind,

Six-thousand strong, to places so remote—
Forbidden places, where I can explore
Dim secrets, complex angles; where I float
In different space-time, learning ghastly lore,
Abominations far beyond their ken.
They think they *have* me in their flimsy den!

THE GODS THROW DICE

I was a traveller on far seas;
I tasted salt on many a breeze.
From land to land,
The hot winds fanned
My lust to find life's inner keys.

In old Khartoum I met a mage—
A wizened and forbidding sage
Who bade me drink.
'Fore I could think,
His potion put me in a rage.

In Xanadu, I told the stars
And read men's fates by Sol and Mars.
Thought I saw deep—
Was blind, asleep
And sealed my findings fast in jars.

Upon the plain of Leng, I rode
'Neath skies where vast dark forces strode;
Searched ever on
And came upon
No inner keys, no secret code.

Now I am old and now I know—
It fills my soul with naught but woe—
The inner key
Is you and me.
The gods throw dice, laugh as they throw.

THE LAST DREAM

(FOR AMBROSE BIERCE)

In dead of night strange tones so drear
Awakened me from dreams of fear.
In my small house above the town,
Unceasing memories dragged me down.
I rose with shivers manifold
That wracked my frame with burning cold.
Some ghastly knowledge full of dread
From out the realms of newly dead
Told me I must go forth to tombs
Where poisoned tree and dark rose blooms.
My soul I sought with peace to calm
And thought of my dead love for balm,
Who in the grave was laid serene
Though fleshless; all about the scene
The moonlight fell as I went forth
To find her gravesite in the north
Upon the solemn secret hill
Where all the night lay hot, lay still.
She beckoned me in voiceless tones
That seemed to waft from baleful stones
In churchyard shadowed dismally;
What could, I thought, *she want with me?*
Of her dark eyes I thought again
And knew we loved—but that was when
She had been living, years ago,
Her lithe and golden frame aglow

With vital force and brimming so
With tender love for me. Then lo!
I reached the grave and bending down
Beheld my love in splendid gown,
Sweet-spiced and perfumed as of yore
Stand slim in roseate ballroom door.
Beheld her in my past mind's eye—
Her bright cheek and her hair like sky
All woven with the circling stars
Like Venus full aligned with Mars.
That time of gleaming spires and domes
When happiness had filled our homes
Was gone; and now fearful tableaux
Alone remained to mock me. Oh,
Of presages and prophecies
And wild winds blowing through stark trees
I'd had my fill; I missed her charms,
Felt but the lack of her sweet arms.
I scrabbled at the filthy earth
And dug beneath to seek new birth.
The dreadful deed was done at length;
Exhausted now was all my strength.
And so beneath gigantic spheres
That orbit heaven through the years
I clasp my skeletonic love;
Forgotten now, my life above.
The moon still gleams, the wind still moans
But we lie here amidst the bones,
Fulfilled at last in death's extreme—
How glorious this long, last dream!

FROM SPECTRAL REALMS

(FOR DONALD WANDREI)

From spectral realms approach the fearful things
Shapen of mystery, forms of cobweb-grey;
I hear the sounds of vast and beating wings.
From out the storm-tossed sky that blots out day,
Long prisoned in declining earthly flesh,
I onward grope through life with feverish eyes
In search of dreamings that may bring some fresh
Insight—or surcease—careless of their guise.

Cessation of existence, special joy—
Devoutly to be wished, as one might say—
And now these *things* grow near; I am their toy.
Their talons grasp me; I have found the way!
These voiceless, faceless, creatures of the grave
Will bring me the cessation that I crave!

MY ASHEN HEART

When from the fragrant earth dim horrors rise,
Dull shadows stipple banks of purple cloud;
The black blood thrums throughout my veins as loud
As screeching cockatoos flock through dark skies.

Now summer's heat has gone and autumn falls:
The quiet dust is sprinkled with dry leaves
And stalks of grass; the coming season heaves
Itself within my brain; belichened walls

Of mute old houses sink in dreary gloom.
Seedpods—maraccas of the twisted trees—
Dance, tremble, rattle; etched on fretting seas—
The season's mist, a dank and dismal spume.

The streetlamps flare aglow like jaundice bright;
Like shrouds of smoke, a chill creeps on my heart
(A tattered wraith that rots and falls apart);
Gone now the summer's shimmer all alight.

Earth's witchery fades deep as summer ebbs,
In silent slumber lies; as I depart
The blackened margins of autumnal webs,
Faint embers die within my ashen heart.

THROUGH DRUID OAKS

With scarlet veins your opalescent robe
Is threaded through; the sacred silver groves
Lie still; the Moon, an iridescent globe
Illumines earth that hides old treasure troves.

Through Druid oaks, their catkins full and wide,
You roam, enraptured, seeking for the shrine
Of Cailleach where sense and soul might guide
Your future way—ill-fated borderline.

Forbidden hungers—feathers of dark wings—
Phantasmal lusts brush on your lips unkissed.
Your breasts are ripe delightsome fruit, that kings
Might pluck from laden boughs with languid wrist.

Now sombre shadows fall and you behold
My dark-robed presence stalking through the wood.
The shadows lengthen, as was long foretold.
Strange melodies ring out, for womanhood.

Your lantern light unmasked and held on high
Now stays my step, as taken unawares,
I find myself held fast 'twixt truth and lie.
Now *who* stalks *who* in answer to *whose* prayers?

Yet still your lithe and lovely limbs' caress
Inflames my body; burning with desire,
Your lips I kiss. To you I acquiesce,
Perfervid; and my veins run with red fire

As in my neck, where beating pulses swell,
(So tempting, yielding, soft) you sink your fangs.
This tryst has proven naught but my death-knell;
Another of *your* daily new birth pangs.

BASILISK EYE

From blue morning sundance to dim twilight dream
The Basilisk broods by the rippling stream.
The bright light gleams forth from its green-golden scales
The warrior hunts it, beholds it and pales.

Through cycles of aeons this grim serpent king
Has ravaged and plundered; the people still sing
Of how from a rooster it hatched from an egg
And grew to be monstrous. The village folk beg

For an end to its slaughter. It slays with a glance
With its Basilisk eye and the warrior's lance
Is no weapon against it, its poisonous breath
So noxious and fatal that mortals meet death.

Its curves are alluring; the people fall prey,
Drawn in by deception. Its camouflage gay
Is blindingly bright. The good townsfolk are led
To regard it with caution lest they should fall dead.

The warrior rides, plated over with mail
That in battle protects him; he cannot now fail.
But his weapon is different. The Basilisk turns
And snarls at the man, as with courage he burns.

This man has been clever—'tis done in a trice!
He holds up a mirror! Another! And thrice,
He circles the monster. And three times at least
The Basilisk's gaze rebounds on the beast!

The serpent is conquered — it falls on its knees.
The warrior triumphs! He drinks to the lees
The sweet cup of victory. The serpent is dead!
No more need the people abide with their dread!

Alchemical powder of Basilisk skin
Is ground up for use by the alchemist's kin.
No longer the villagers live at dire risk
Of death from the monster — the feared Basilisk!

DEAD PALE MOON

(FOR NORA MAY FRENCH)

Bright day is done with all its work of gleaming,
And vanished now the dewdrops crystal-seeming;
Dim forest depths grow steeped in dusky glooms;
The flowers gold and green close all their blooms.

The placid pool, draped 'round by weeping willows,
Is rippled by chill winds' uprising billows—
Serene no more. The rains send silver ringing
Upon black earth as startled birds go winging.

The crimson kiss of sunset now subsiding
Lends twilight's arch a bloody tinge abiding
And all day's woven, wondrous, lustrous threads
Flee glimmering and surging, torn in shreds.

Now creep the blacks and purples slowly shifting
'Neath spectral silent Maiden whitely lifting.
Can face so pocked and leering prove a boon?
Fall to your knees before the dead pale Moon!

ELDER BEINGS

They came across abysses from doomed planes
Unutterably distant, far from ken
Of human beings writhing in their pain
Of mortal life—mere women and mere men.

They fled their crumbling towers and citadels
In search of living planets for their use
And—so Alhazred's secret mad book tells—
They flocked and settled on the Earth, let loose

To rave and raven. Human minds succumbed
To alien thought-forms of these Elder Things.
Through fevered dreams their dreadful visions thrummed,
These creatures with their terrible black wings.

And so at last it was that humankind
Obliterated, lived and thrived no more.
The Elder Beings in their might combined
Had shattered human life—so tells the lore!

A DYING FALL

A dying fall my deathsong makes
As here I lie on my last bed;
A dying fall my deathsong makes;
No doubt that I will soon be dead.

Red blossoms at the window grow;
White blossoms spread beneath the trees,
As here I lie but soon must go.
I drank my fill of life—the lees

Are all that's left and now the glass
Of wine is all but fully spent.
A dying fall; my life must pass;
And others tell what this has meant.

EMERALDESSE

As though from some gem-crusted world—
Far distant, circling dark-hued skies
Whose limits are by gods unfurled—
I see the walls that do arise
In Emeraldesse, fair citadel,
When it stood proud, before it fell.

Within the walls of Emeraldesse
The banners flutter in the breeze.
Its soldiers march; its priests confess
And sail on fate-predestined seas.
In Emeraldesse, fair citadel
There falls a note, there tolls a bell.

The heavy-throated bells peal slow,
Toll ever on in Emeraldesse—
Its fairness flown, its faery glow
Half-vanished now beneath the stress
Of warring kingdoms that do press
Upon the bounds of Emeraldesse.

Red flaring sunsets round the walls
And towers so proud; with such largesse
Endow the endless darkling halls;
So princes live in Emeraldesse.
But ruined now, its antique charms—
For you have fled my clasping arms.

In Emeraldesse you seek to find
Sweet life without me, but I know
That which you seek will only bind—
Your mind dark seeds begins to grow.
And ghastly shapes around you press;
Your life will end—in Emeraldesse.

BLACK PILGRIMAGE

A blotch of red obscures the mournful moon;
The chilling air wafts inland from the coast;
Old Providence lies silent as a ghost;
The pilgrimage, I fear, has come too soon—

Black pilgrimage of worshippers who are
Devoted to unholy doings here,
Their robes worm-clotted; at this time of year,
They gather to perform their rites bizarre.
And as they wind their wicked way along
The downward path, I know that *all is wrong*.

SOULS OF SAMHAIN

When harvest ends and first frost's on the land
The Souls of Samhain show their spirit hand.
From summer pastures cattle are brought in,
Livestock are slaughtered; let winter begin!

Light up the hilltop bonfires! Feasts commence!
On All Souls' Night, the goblins hasten hence,
Revisiting their homes and living kin;
Dead Otherworldly souls scream, wail and din.

Since Tigernmas, the King to Crom Cruach,
Did sacrifice a child in horror stark,
Did smash its newborn head 'gainst idol-stone
To safeguard people, wintry land and throne,

The Souls of Samhain still we must appease—
Scatter the blackened ashes, if you please!
From winter's darkness and its dread decay
Bright bonfires, like the Sun, protect the day.

Some welcome dining places don't forget,
And candles in your westward windows set
For Souls of Samhain who appear this night;
Use salt and iron should they give you fright.

This *danse macabre* will hear the churchbells ring.
Let's feast with apples, nuts and everything!
Let's go in guise unto our neighbours' doors
With painted, veiled faces—Samhain's laws!

With decorated horse-skulls let us mum
Now that the year's dark half has swiftly come!
Let's take our cattle killed and freeze our meat
So through grim winter's length we still can eat!

The Souls of Samhain—do they mean us harm?
Appease them and the restless spirits calm.
The *Aos Si* will soon depart this earth;
Let's cheer them on their way with festive mirth!

THE WAVES OF FEAR

When from the dark there wash the waves of fear
That lave my soul with terrible deep chill,
Forebodings fill me—things that leap and leer.
Throughout this dismal round that forms the year,
The crawling horrors make my soul so ill,
When from the dark there wash the waves of fear.

At midnight leprous, spectral horrors steer
And steal into my home, shudders instill;
Forebodings fill me—things that leap and leer.

My laugh maniacal from there to here
Is heard upon the night-winds near the mill
When from the dark there wash the waves of fear

My mind is cracked, and at itself doth jeer;
It seems a fiendish croucher haunts the sill;
Forebodings fill me—things that leap and leer.

How can I quell disquiet's fraught frontier,
And can I hope to find the strength of will
When from the dark there wash the waves of fear?
Forebodings fill me—things that leap and leer.

POETRY ACKNOWLEDGMENTS

The following poems first appeared as follows:

"The Adverse Star" in *Spectral Realms* No 4 (Winter 2016)

"When the Nightwind Howls" in *Spectral Realms* No 10 (Winter 2019)

"The Silent Silver Sea" in *Spectral Realms* No 12 (Winter 2020)

"Shadowlands" in *Spectral Realms* No 14 (Winter 2021)

"The Witches' Bower" in *The Small Tapestry* (Spring 2018) and in *Spectral Realms* No 10 (Winter 2019)

"Time's Vulture" in *Spectral Realms* No 12 (Winter 2020)

"Frozen Voices" in *Spectral Realms* No 13 (Summer 2020)

"The Boneless" in *Spectral Realms* No 19 (Summer 2023)

"The Night is Black and White" in *Spectral Realms* No 2 (Winter 2015)

"The Golden Diadem" in *Spectral Realms* No 3 (Summer 2015)

"Under the Tuscan Moon" in *Spectral Realms* No 6 (Winter 2017)

"My Ashen Heart" in *Spectral Realms* No 2 (Winter 2015)

"Through Druid Oaks" in *Spectral Realms* No 8 (Winter 2018)

"From Spectral Realms" in *Spectral Realms* No 10 (Winter 2019)

"Dead Pale Moon" in *Spectral Realms* 3 (Summer 2015)

"Elder Beings" in George Wilhite (ed). *Beyond the Cosmic Veil*. Barbwire Butterfly Press, 2015, and in *Spectral Realms* No 6 (Winter 2017)

"The Waves of Fear" in *Spectral Realms* 5 (Summer 2016)

"Souls of Samhain" in *Spectral Realms* (Winter 2016) and in [Steve Lines, ed], *Hallowe'en Howlings*, [2017].

"The Last Dream" in *Weird Fiction Review* No 4 (Fall 2013)

"Doomed Cassilda" in *Cyaegha* No 13 (Spring 2015)

"The Fantastic Flame" in *Penumbra* No 1 (2020)

"The Tongueless Dead" in *Spectral Realms* No 13 (Summer 2020)

"Basilisk Eye" in *Penumbra* No 2 (2021)

"Lamia" and "Ice Demons" in Frank Coffman (ed).*Speculations #3: Poetry from the Weird Poets Society Facebook Group from 2020*. Mind's Eye Publications, 2021

The following poems first appeared in *Sharnoth's Spores and Other Seeds*. Calne, Wiltshire UK: Rainfall Books, October 2010: "Like Scarlet Wine," "Lines on a Drawing By Hannes Bok," "Phantom Lover," "The Goblin Goblet," "The Gods Throw Dice," "Emeraldesse," "Searcher," "In Splendour All Arrayed." "The Goblin Goblet" also appeared in *Weird Fiction Review No 1* (Fall 2010).

The following poems appear here for the first time:

"Shoggoths"
"With Wizard Way"
"Azathoth, or: The Daemon-Sultan"
"Alchemy of Oblivion"
"Shub-Niggurath"
"The Loathly God"
"A Dream of Kamog"
"Love's Ruin"
"A Dying Fall"
"Black Pilgrimage"

AUTHOR BIOGRAPHY

Rhysling and Australian Shadows Awards-nominated poet, musician, writer and occultist **Leigh Blackmore** (BCA Writing, Hons, Univ Wollongong) debuted in weird verse aged 15 with a Lovecraftian sonnet published in R. Alain Everts' journal *The Arkham Sampler* (new series, 1984). His fantastic poetry has been widely published in magazines and anthologies including *Anno Klarkash-Ton, Cyaegha, Beyond the Cosmic Veil, Songs of the Shattered World: The Broken Hymns of Hastur, Penumbra, Spectral Realms*, and *Weird Fiction Review*.

Reviewing his verse collection *Spores from Sharnoth & Other Madnesses* (P'rea Press, 2008; 3rd reprint 2013; variant ed as *Sharnoth's Spores & Other Seeds*, Rainfall Books, 2010) *Dead Reckonings* (for which Leigh reviews regularly) declared him "One of the leading weird poets of our era."

Leigh resides in the Illawarra NSW, where he ran his own editorial business, Proof Perfect, for over a decade. Dubbed 'Mr Horror' by the Australian press, and a past President of the Australian Horror Writers Association, Leigh edited for AHWA *Midnight Echo,* Issue 5 (2011). He formerly edited *Terror Australis* magazine (1987-92) and its subsequent book anthology (1993) and is a four-time Ditmar Award nominee (once for fiction and thrice for criticism).

He is currently seeking a publisher for his debut novel, and assembling an edition of Robert Bloch's *Selected Letters*. His collection of weird fiction, *Nightmare Logic*, is forthcoming from IFWG Australia.